Wylie

by Iain Gray

WRITING *to* REMEMBER

WRITING *to* REMEMBER

79 Main Street, Newtongrange,
Midlothian EH22 4NA
Tel: 0131 344 0414
E-mail: info@lang-syne.co.uk
www.langsyneshop.co.uk

Design by Dorothy Meikle
Printed by Printwell Ltd
© Lang Syne Publishers Ltd 2023

All rights reserved. No part of this publication may be reproduced, stored or introduced into a retrieval system, or transmitted in any form or by any means (electronic, mechanical, photocopying, recording or otherwise) without the prior written permission of Lang Syne Publishers Ltd.

ISBN 978-1-85217-776-8

Wylie

MOTTO:
Trust

CREST:
A hound

TERRITORIES:
Loch Lomond, Caithness, Sutherland

NAME variations include:
Wiley
Wilie
Whyley
Wyley
Wyllie

Chapter one:

The origins of the clan system

by Rennie McOwan

The original Scottish clans of the Highlands and the great families of the Lowlands and Borders were gatherings of families, relatives, allies and neighbours for mutual protection against rivals or invaders.

Scotland experienced invasion from the Vikings, the Romans and English armies from the south. The Norman invasion of what is now England also had an influence on land-holding in Scotland. Some of these invaders stayed on and in time became 'Scottish'.

The word clan derives from the Gaelic language term 'clann', meaning children, and it was first used many centuries ago as communities were formed around tribal lands in glens and mountain fastnesses.

The format of clans changed over the centuries, but at its best the chief and his family held the land on behalf of all, like trustees, and the ordinary clansmen and women believed they had a blood relationship with the founder of their clan.

There were two way duties and obligations. An inadequate chief could be deposed and replaced by someone of greater ability.

Clan people had an immense pride in race. Their relationship with the chief was like adult children to a father and they had a real dignity.

The concept of clanship is very old and a more feudal notion of authority gradually crept in.

Pictland, for instance, was divided into seven principalities ruled by feudal leaders who were the strongest and most charismatic leaders of their particular groups.

By the sixth century the 'British' kingdoms of Strathclyde, Lothian and Celtic Dalriada (Argyll) had emerged and Scotland, as one nation, began to take shape in the time of King Kenneth MacAlpin.

Some chiefs claimed descent from ancient kings which may not have been accurate in every case.

By the twelfth and thirteenth centuries the clans and families were more strongly brought under the central control of Scottish monarchs.

Lands were awarded and administered more and more under royal favour, yet the power of the area clan chiefs was still very great.

The long wars to ensure Scotland's

independence against the expansionist ideas of English monarchs extended the influence of some clans and reduced the lands of others.

Those who supported Scotland's greatest king, Robert the Bruce, were awarded the territories of the families who had opposed his claim to the Scottish throne.

In the Scottish Borders country – the notorious Debatable Lands – the great families built up a ferocious reputation for providing warlike men accustomed to raiding into England and occasionally fighting one another.

Chiefs had the power to dispense justice and to confiscate lands and clan warfare produced a society where martial virtues – courage, hardiness, tenacity – were greatly admired.

Gradually the relationship between the clans and the Crown became strained as Scottish monarchs became more orientated to life in the Lowlands and, on occasion, towards England.

The Highland clans spoke a different language, Gaelic, whereas the language of Lowland Scotland and the court was Scots and in more modern times, English.

Highlanders dressed differently, had different

customs, and their wild mountain land sometimes seemed almost foreign to people living in the Lowlands.

It must be emphasised that Gaelic culture was very rich and story-telling, poetry, piping, the clarsach (harp) and other music all flourished and were greatly respected.

Highland culture was different from other parts of Scotland but it was not inferior or less sophisticated.

Central Government, whether in London or Edinburgh, sometimes saw the Gaelic clans as a challenge to their authority and some sent expeditions into the Highlands and west to crush the power of the Lords of the Isles.

Nevertheless, when the eighteenth century Jacobite Risings came along the cause of the Stuarts was mainly supported by Highland clans.

The word Jacobite comes from the Latin for James – Jacobus. The Jacobites wanted to restore the exiled Stuarts to the throne of Britain.

The monarchies of Scotland and England became one in 1603 when King James VI of Scotland (1st of England) gained the English throne after Queen Elizabeth died.

The origins of the clan system

The Union of Parliaments of Scotland and England, the Treaty of Union, took place in 1707.

Some Highland clans, of course, and Lowland families opposed the Jacobites and supported the incoming Hanoverians.

After the Jacobite cause finally went down at Culloden in 1746 a kind of ethnic cleansing took place. The power of the chiefs was curtailed. Tartan and the pipes were banned in law.

Many emigrated, some because they wanted to, some because they were evicted by force. In addition, many Highlanders left for the cities of the south to seek work.

Many of the clan lands became home to sheep and deer shooting estates.

But the warlike traditions of the clans and the great Lowland and Border families lived on, with their descendants fighting bravely for freedom in two world wars.

Remember the men from whence you came, says the Gaelic proverb, and to that could be added the role of many heroic women

The spirit of the clan, of having roots, whether Highland or Lowland, means much to thousands of people.

Meanwhile, many families proudly boast the heraldic device known as a Coat of Arms, as featured on our front cover.

The central motif of the Coat of Arms would originally have been what was sometimes borne on the shield of a warrior to distinguish himself from others on the battlefield.

Not featured on the Coat of Arms, but highlighted on page three, is the family motto and related crest – with the latter frequently different from the central motif.

Clan warfare produced a society where courage and tenacity were greatly admired

Chapter two:

Fame and distinction

A name with a number of possible points of origin, 'Wylie' and its spelling variants became popular as a surname, in common with many others, in the aftermath of the Norman Conquest of England in 1066 and subsequent spread of Anglo-Norman influence throughout the rest of the British Isles.

Previous to this, many people were identified in relation to a number of factors including where they lived, their occupation or physical characteristics.

One explanation of the origin of the Wylie name is that it springs from 'wile', or 'wyle', denoting 'sly' or 'crafty', as in a fox.

As a locational name, it possibly stems from the Old English 'wilig', indicating 'willow' and 'leah', denoting either a water meadow or cleared area in a wood or forest.

As a place name 'Willey' is common throughout England in the modern-day counties of Warwickshire, Devonshire, Surrey, Cheshire, Herefordshire and Shropshire.

In Scotland, however, the consensus is that it stems from a pet form of the popular forename 'William'.

Also in Scotland, the name is said to have first appeared in Dumfriesshire, in the southwest, and this holds out the interesting prospect that the ancestors of those who would adopt it were part of the Brittonic (British) Kingdom of Strathclyde, known in the Cumbric tongue as *Teyrnas Ystrad Clut* and which flourished from the fifth century to approximately 1030.

Known by the Welsh as *Hen Ogledd* – the Old North – this vast kingdom embraced northern England and southern Scotland and was also known as *Alt Clut*, from a Brittonic term for the fortress of Dumbarton Rock, the main powerbase.

Having developed during the post-Roman period, the kingdom was originally home to the Brythonic tribe the Damnonii and appears to have become known as 'Strathclyde' – the 'strath' or 'valley' of the River Clyde – when its centre of power shifted to what is now the Govan area of Glasgow following the sacking of the rock by the Vikings in 870.

In some cases, bearers of a particular surname are recognised as having kinship with more than one clan, because the name was not necessarily confined to a single territory.

This is the case with the Wylies, who share kinship as a sept, or sub-branch, of Clan Macfarlane and Clan Gunn, both of whom also have 'MacWilliam' ('son of William') as a sept – with 'Wylie', as previously noted, a pet form of 'William.'

Derived from the Gaelic *clanna*, meaning 'children', a clan was a close-knit tribal grouping settled in a particular territory and whose members – or 'children', or 'kin' – owed unswerving loyalty to a chief who, in turn, was bound by duty and honour to protect them.

Not all members of a clan necessarily shared the same surname as the chief – known as *ceann-cinnidh*, meaning 'head and chief of the family' – and these 'kindred of the clan', or 'kinsfolk', were recognised, as they are to this day, as septs of the clan.

As such, they are entitled to share in its heritage and traditions that include the right to display its tartan and heraldry of crest and motto – this recognised by the Lord Lyon King of Arms of Scotland, the final arbiter on all matters heraldic.

With their heartland the western shores of

Loch Lomond upwards of Tarbet, the Macfarlanes have the motto 'This I'll defend' and crest a demi-savage wielding a sword and holding a crown.

Clan Gunn, whose territories included Caithness, Sutherland and the Orkney Isles, boast the motto 'Either peace or war' and crest of an arm with the hand brandishing a sword.

But, in common with others who are regarded as septs of a clan, the Wylies also have their own proud heraldic motto and crest – devised at some indeterminate date for a prominent family of the name and now shared by all bearers.

For the Wylies, the motto is 'Fides', which translates as 'Trust' and the crest features a hound.

But it was much further afield, in Russia, that one eighteenth century bearer of the name stamped an indelible mark on the historical record as a pioneering physician and surgeon whose contributions to medicine are recognised to this day.

Referred to in Russia as Yakov Vassilievich Villiye, he was much better known in his native Tulliallan, near Kincardine, as James Wylie and, after he had gained international fame and acclaim, as Sir James Wylie, 1st Baronet.

Born in 1768, the son of a church minister and

the second of five children, he was apprenticed to a local doctor before studying medicine at the University of Edinburgh from 1786 to 1789.

Invited to Russia when aged only 22 by fellow Scot Dr James Rogerson, a court physician to Catherine the Great, this was at a time when a number of Scots medical men such as Dr Rogerson and Dr Thomas Garvie had already distinguished themselves because of their expertise.

James Wylie, however, was destined to achieve not only great personal distinction but also make a valuable and enduring contribution to Russia's entire medical system.

The country he had arrived in was vastly different from his native Scotland, and not only in size.

A total autocracy, where serfdom prevailed, it was under the tyrannical grip of Catherine the Great.

But she had recognised the need for her backward nation to be radically overhauled – not so much in terms of the social condition of the majority of its huge population, but in commerce and technology and she actively encouraged the importation of Western skills.

Four years after his arrival, Wylie reached the rank of senior surgeon in the elite Eletsky Regiment and this early experience in military medicine would prove to serve both he and his adopted nation well in later years.

In 1795 he was appointed a physician to the Russian court after saving the life of the Dutch ambassador after attempts by other doctors had failed.

Four years later, it was through another failure on the part of fellow doctors that Wylie drew even closer to the royal household.

A close personal friend of Tsar Paul I, who had succeeded Catherine, had taken seriously ill and all attempts to save him were proving fruitless – until Wylie performed a delicate operation involving the first tracheotomy performed in Russia.

A grateful Paul immediately appointed Yakov Vassilievich Villiye, as he was now known, as his personal physician. He would go on to serve in the post to yet another two tsars – Alexander I and Nicholas I.

Referring to the tracheotomy he had performed, Wylie would later joke how he owed his fame to 'cutting a man's throat'.

Alexander I, successor to Paul, enjoyed a particularly close relationship with Wylie and actively encouraged him in his innovative plans for the better administration of the nation's medical system.

In 1804, he became founder and president of the Medical Academy of St Petersburg and Moscow, a post he held for thirty years while, two years later, he was appointed Inspector General of the Army Board of Health and, in 1812, during Napoleon's invasion of Russia, directed the medical department of the Ministry of War.

Present seven years before in Austria at the battle of Austerlitz – one of Napoleon's greatest victories – he had been shocked at the primitive and inhumane treatment of the Russian wounded by their own side.

Wyle put an end to this practice, so that by the time of the battle of Borodino in September of 1812, not only Russian but also enemy wounded received the best care that could be provided under the horrific circumstances.

In September of 1840, marking the anniversary of Borodino – which had proved a pyrrhic victory for the French with enormous casualties on both sides – Tsar Nicholas I had a special medal struck bearing a profile of Wylie on one side, while he is also featured as a character in Tolstoy's epic novel *War and Peace*.

Writing to Wylie on the occasion, the tsar said: "I cannot but call to mind the services which you rendered on that memorable epoch when, at the head of the corps of medical and surgical officers of the army, you yourself ceased not to give a grand example of zeal and self-denial for the welfare and relief of suffering warriors."

Napoleon awarded him the Legion d'Honneur for his role in treating wounded French soldiers, while he also received honours from other combatant nations Prussia, Austria and Italy.

In 1814, he accompanied Alexander on a visit to Britain when he was knighted and given a baronetcy – his proud relatives coming down from Kincardine to witness the event at Ascot.

Alexander died in 1825, to be succeeded by Nicholas I, who also gave Wylie free reign to modernise the country's health system.

Among his many accomplishments were the introduction of proper examinations for doctors, the regular and rigorous inspection of hospitals, the setting up of a system of medical case records and the establishment of medical schools.

He was also one of the earliest doctors to recognise the curative effect of sunlight on patients – noting the recovery rate of those in well-lit hospital wards was four times greater than in poorly-lit ones.

Aged 86, Yakov Vassilievich Villiye died in 1854 and was buried in St Petersburg in the presence of Nicholas I and the royal family.

A bachelor, he left his fortune to the Russian nation to be used to build a hospital in St Petersburg.

Now the centre of medical excellence the Medical and Surgical Academy of St Petersburg, a statue of Wylie adorns its courtyard while, in his native land, James Wylie Place in Kincardine is named in his honour.

Sir James Wylie, Ist Baronet

Chapter three:

Codebreakers and translators

One bearer of the Wylie name who made a significant contribution to the secret war that helped defeat Nazi Germany, was the mathematician and codebreaker Shaun Wylie.

Born in Oxford in 1913, a son of the noted Oxford University academic and administrator Sir Francis Wylie, in 1940 he was invited by Alan Turing, head of codebreaking activities at Bletchley Park, Buckinghamshire, to join the 'Hut 8' section.

This unit worked on the Enigma coding machine that was used by the German Navy, and Wylie became head of one of the hut's sub-sections.

Of his achievements, Hugh Alexander, who succeeded Turing as head of Hut 8, said: "Except for Turing, no-one made a bigger contribution to the success of Hut 8 than Shaun Wylie.

"He was astonishingly quick and resourceful and contributed to theory and practice in a number of different directions."

Appointed chief mathematician in 1958 at GCHQ, the UK's signals intelligence operation at Cheltenham, and involved in research in the arcane world of public-key cryptography, he died in 2009 after also having been instrumental in the world of politics in the foundation of the Liberal Democrats Party.

Through his parentage, and in the much different world of sport, as a young man he had also qualified to play international hockey for Scotland.

His son Keith Wylie, born in 1945, also displayed a talent for sport – in his case as a croquet player.

Winner of the Men's Championship in 1968, the Open Championship in 1970 and 1971, and winning twice while representing Great Britain, he also wrote *Croquet Tactics*, considered the definitive book on the game. An inductee of the World Croquet Federation Hall of Fame, he died in 1999.

Two other bearers of the Wylie name gained distinction through their breaking of the complexities of the Chinese and Tibetan languages.

Born in London in 1815 but raised in the Scottish town of Drumlithie, Kincardineshire, Alexander Wylie was the Protestant missionary who translated ancient Chinese works on mathematics, mechanics and astronomy.

But a career as a missionary and linguist had not been his original intention, having been apprenticed for a time as a cabinet maker.

By chance, he came across a Chinese grammar book that had been translated not into English, but Latin – and he determined to master this as a first step towards understanding Chinese.

Proving a natural linguist, this he duly did and, as a devout Christian and in recognition of his language skills, in 1846 he was posted by the London Missionary Society to Shanghai to superintend its missionary work.

This primarily involved overseeing and completing the distribution of one million New Testaments translated into Chinese, while from 1863 he was also an agent of the British and Foreign Bible Society.

But his main contribution was through his scholarship in Chinese culture and language, including the discovery that solutions to a number of mathematical equations had been known to the Chinese in much earlier times than had previously been thought.

Also translating scientific work and gospels from English into Chinese and author of the noted 1835 work *Jottings on the Science of the Chinese*, he died in 1887.

Renowned for his scholarship and advancement of knowledge in the West of Tibetan language and culture, Dr Turrell Verl Wylie, more familiarly known as Terry Wylie, was born in 1927 in Durango, Colorado.

A professor of Tibetan Studies at Washington University and first chair of its department of Asian language and literature, he is best known for his translation technique known as the Wylie transliteration.

Following China's invasion and annexation of Tibet in 1948, he was instrumental in a number of Tibetan refugees finding refuge in the United States.

He died in 1984, while the Dalai Lama said of him: "Dr Wylie's strong and genuine feelings for the Tibetan people and their just cause will long remain deeply appreciated.

"In the death of Dr Wylie we have lost a true friend and a distinguished scholar of Tibetan studies."

In contemporary science Peter Wylie, born in London in 1930, is the renowned expert on the origin, structure and composition of rocks and the properties of the semi-molten material known as magma.

Having held a number of academic posts including, from 1983 until his retirement in 1999, professor of geology at the California Institute of Technology, he is the author of a number of definitive textbooks on his fields of study.

These include *The Dynamic Earth*, first published in 1971 and, from 1976, *The Way the Earth Works*, while he is also noted for his contributions on earth sciences in the *Encyclopaedia Britannica*.

A former president of the International Union of Geodesy and Geophysics (IUGG), his many honours include the Wollaston Medal of the Geological Society of London and the Roebling Medal of the Mineralogical Society of America.

The title of his best-selling book *The Dynamic Earth*, meanwhile, lends its name to the top interactive visitor attraction Dynamic Earth, situated at the foot of the Salisbury Crags, Edinburgh and a similar attraction in Ontario, Canada.

Bearers of the Wylie and Wyllie names have also excelled in the highly creative world of art.

Recognised as the most distinguished maritime artist of his day, William Lionel Wyllie was born in London in 1851 but spent a great deal of his early years with his parents in France.

His father William Morrison Wyllie was an artist and he encouraged his son to also take up the palette.

Studying in London under noted painters including John Everett Millais and Edwin Henry Landseer, his talents were such that when aged only eighteen he won the prestigious Turner Gold Medal for his painting *Dawn after a Storm*.

Fascinated by the sea, he concentrated on maritime themes and his most famous work is the 42ft (13m) panorama *Battle of Trafalgar*, now on display in the Royal Naval Museum, Portsmouth.

Also noted for other subjects including *Battle of the Nile* and HMS *Good Hope* and a founder member of the Society for Nautical Research, he died in 1931 and was buried with full naval honours – a year after *Battle of Trafalgar* was unveiled by King George V.

In contemporary art, Rose Wylie, born in Kent in 1934, is the English painter noted for her striking work of extremely large paintings executed on un-stretched, un-primed canvas.

Winner of the 2011 Paul Hamlyn Foundation

Prize for Visual Arts, she was married to fellow painter Roy Oxlade, who died in 2014.

Renowned for a number of open-air works of art, George Wyllie was the Scottish artist and sculptor born in 1921 in the Shettleston district of Glasgow.

Having worked as a customs officer in Gourock before taking up art full-time, his many eye-catching works included *Straw Locomotive*, a full-size steam locomotive fashioned from straw that was suspended from the Finnieston Crane, on the banks of the River Clyde, Glasgow.

Dominating the Clydeside skyline for a number of months throughout 1987, it was then returned to the former Springburn locomotive works, where it was constructed, and ceremonially burnt.

Other Wyllie creations include the *Clyde Clock* – 'the clock on running legs' outside the city's Buchanan Street bus station – while his *Monument to Maternity*, in the form of a giant nappy pin, is on the site of the city's former Rottenrow Maternity Hospital.

The recipient of an MBE and a president of the Society of Scottish Artists, he died in 2012.

Chapter four:

On the world stage

From the stage and literature to politics and enterprise, bearers of the Wylie name and its spelling variants have achieved fame and acclaim.

Active in the world of entertainment from an early age, **Adam Wylie** is the American actor, voice actor and singer born in 1984 in San Dimas, California.

With big screen credits including the 2005 *Rebound* and, from the same year, *American Pie Presents: Band Camp*, his voice acting credits include the 1994 *The Swan Princess* and the 1996 *All Dogs Go to Heaven 2*.

The recipient of a Young Artists Award for his voice acting in the animated series *Dennis the Menace*, he appeared on Broadway in the Tony Award-winning revival of *Into the Woods*.

Also on American shores, **Samira Wiley** is the actress known for her role from 2013 to 2019 of Poussey Washington in the Netflix comedy-drama series *Orange is the New Black* and, from 2017, as Moira in *The Handmaid's Tale*.

Born in 1987 in Washington, D.C., her other

film credits include the 2011 *The Sitter* and, from 2018, *Social Animals*.

From the stage to the highly competitive world of sport, **Douglas Wyllie** is the Scottish former rugby union player who, making his international debut in 1984 as a fly-half against Australia, earned eighteen caps playing for his country.

Born in Edinburgh in 1963 and a former captain of Stewarts Melville RFC, he has also coached in New Zealand and, back on home turf, for Kirkcaldy RFC.

Taking to the heavens, **Charles Wylie** was the American astronomer and leading authority on meteors and meteorites born in 1886 in Cedar Rapids, Iowa.

Having worked for a time at the U.S. Naval Observatory, Washington and the University of Illinois Observatory, it was along with fellow astronomer Frank Whittle that in the 1930s he studied the origins of meteors.

The first vice-president of the Society for Research on Meteorites, now the Meteoritical Society, he died in 1976.

Bearers of the Wylie name have also excelled in the creative world of literature.

Born in 1885 in Melbourne, Australia into a

rather dysfunctional family – her father having fled his native Scotland to escape creditors – Ida Alex Ross Wylie was the novelist, poet and campaigner for women's rights better knows as **I. A. R. Wylie**.

Settling in London and, based on the knowledge of a friend who had experienced life in India, she penned a series of books based on the sub-continent including the 1910 *The Rajah's People* and the 1916 *The Hermit Doctor of Gaya*.

Living for a time in Germany, she wrote books including her 1911 *Rambles in the Black Forest*, while joining the suffragette movement when returning to London and working for a time as 'sub-editor and bottle washer' with *The Suffragette* publication.

Eventually settling in Hollywood, many of her novels were adapted for screen including the 1942 *Keeper of the Flame*, starring Katharine Hepburn and Spencer Tracy; she died in 1959.

Author of a play, a television adaptation of which is listed by the *Guinness Book of Records* as the most frequently repeated programme ever, Maurice Laurence Samuelson Metzenberg was the English playwright better known by his pen name **Lauri Wylie**.

Born in Southport in 1880, a brother of the

theatrical agent Julian Samuelson, the early film pioneer G.B. Samuelson and uncle of the former British Film Commissioner Sydney Samuelson, his short play *Dinner for One* was first performed at the Prince of Wales Theatre, London, in 1934.

Despite its popularity, he never benefited financially from its later script rights – these having been sold to the comedian Freddy Frinton who starred in the 1963 television adaptation.

For reasons perhaps best known to Germans themselves, this adaptation has proven an annual hit for more than fifty years with their television viewers when screened over the festive period.

Wylie, unaware how popular *Dinner for One* was destined to become, died in poverty in 1951 – living in the camper van that had become his home.

In a much different writing genre, **Philip Wylie**, born in 1902 in Beverley, Massachusetts, was the best-selling American author of science fiction and works on ecology and the threat of nuclear warfare.

Author of works including the 1939 *Gladiator*, part-inspiration for the *Superman* comic book hero and co-author with Edwin Balmer of the 1933 *When Worlds Collide*, inspiration for the comic strip *Flash Gordon* and adapted for the film of the name in 1951, his interests also embraced physics, biology and psychology.

Only a few months before the first successful atomic bomb test at Alamogordo, New Mexico, on July 16, 1945 – the most highly classified secret of the Second World War – he was placed under house arrest by the FBI.

This was because, unwittingly, the plot of the novel he was writing, *The Paradise Crater*, envisioned a post-war Nazi conspiracy to develop nuclear bombs.

Later an adviser to the chairman of the Joint Congressional Committee for Atomic Energy, he died in 1971.

In contemporary times, **Andrew Wylie** is the American literary agent known in the book industry as 'The Jackal.' Born in 1947 in New York City, he founded the Andrew Wyle literary agency in his native city in 1980, opening another office sixteen years later in London.

Now representing more than 1,000 authors including Martin Amis and Salman Rushdie and estates including that of Saul Bellow, he acquired his nickname because of his success in 'poaching' clients from other agencies.

In the world of music, Richard Wayne Wylie,

born in 1939 in Detroit, was the American pianist, bandleader, singer, songwriter and record producer better known as **Popcorn Wylie**.

Associated with the legendary Motown Records in its early years and, with his band Popcorn and the Mohawks releasing singles including *Custer's Last Man* he also played piano on the 1961 hit by the Miracles *Shop Around*, in addition to best-selling recordings by other artistes; he died in 2008.

In the world of politics, **Norman Wylie**, more formally known as Lord Wylie, was the British Conservative and Scottish Unionist politician born in Elderslie, Renfrewshire in 1923.

Having served as Member of Parliament (MP) for Edinburgh Pentlands between 1964 and 1974 and in the posts of Lord Advocate and also Solicitor General for Scotland, he died in 2005.

In the realms of contemporary Scottish justice, Alexander Wylie is the judge of the Supreme Courts of Scotland titled as **Lord Kinclaven**.

Born in 1951 and qualifying as a solicitor in 1976, he has served as a member of the Scottish Criminal Cases Review Commission and was appointed a judge of the Court of Session and High Court of Justiciary in 2005.

While many bearers of the Wylie name and its spelling variants that include 'Wiley' have achieved distinction, others have acquired notoriety.

On November 24, 1990, the normally placid American community of Thermopolis, Wyoming, was stunned to learn that three of its townsfolk had been blasted to death by a shotgun.

The perpetrator was 15-year-old **James Wiley** who, after an argument with his stepmother Becky Wiley, shot her and three of his brothers, including 10-year-old Willy, before setting the family's mobile home ablaze.

Quickly apprehended, he was soon charged and, despite his age, tried as an adult.

Changing his original plea of innocent by reason of mental illness, he later changed it to guilty of three counts of first-degree murder, one count of second-degree murder and arson.

Sentenced to three life sentences and one 20-years-to-life sentence, to run concurrently, plus 18 to 20 years for arson, he was confined in Wyoming State Penitentiary.

In 1995, however, he managed to escape and was on the run for 72 hours before being caught.